DARING AND DANGEROUS

# STORM CHASERS

KEVIN WALKER

ROURKE
Educational Media

rourkeeducationalmedia.com

# Before, During, and After Reading Activities

## Before Reading: Building Background Knowledge and Academic Vocabulary

"Before Reading" strategies activate prior knowledge and set a purpose for reading. Before reading a book, it is important to tap into what your child or students already know about the topic. This will help them develop their vocabulary and increase their reading comprehension.

**Questions and activities to build background knowledge:**
1. *Look at the cover of the book. What will this book be about?*
2. *What do you already know about the topic?*
3. *Let's study the Table of Contents. What will you learn about in the book's chapters?*
4. *What would you like to learn about this topic? Do you think you might learn about it from this book? Why or why not?*

### Building Academic Vocabulary

Building academic vocabulary is critical to understanding subject content.
Assist your child or students to gain meaning of the following vocabulary words.

**Content Area Vocabulary**

Read the list. What do these words mean?

- *cluster*
- *cockpit*
- *diameter*
- *evacuate*
- *measurement*
- *radar*

## During Reading: Writing Component

"During Reading" strategies help to make connections, monitor understanding, generate questions, and stay focused.
1. *While reading, write in your reading journal any questions you have or anything you do not understand.*
2. *After completing each chapter, write a summary of the chapter in your reading journal.*
3. *While reading, make connections with the text and write them in your reading journal.*
   a) *Text to Self – What does this remind me of in my life? What were my feelings when I read this?*
   b) *Text to Text – What does this remind me of in another book I've read? How is this different from other books I've read?*
   c) *Text to World – What does this remind me of in the real world? Have I heard about this before? (News, current events, school, etc....)*

## After Reading: Comprehension and Extension Activity

"After Reading" strategies provide an opportunity to summarize, question, reflect, discuss, and respond to text. After reading the book, work on the following questions with your child or students to check their level of reading comprehension and content mastery.
1. *Why do storm chasers track extreme weather? (Summarize)*
2. *How can early warning systems help people in extreme weather situations? (Infer)*
3. *Why do hurricane hunters fly into hurricanes? (Asking Questions)*
4. *Have you experienced an extreme weather event? What was it like? (Text to Self Connection)*

**Extension Activity**

Almost everyone has a story about living through extreme weather such as a tornado, hurricane, thunderstorm or blizzard. Ask your family members about their experiences. Write these stories to create a family book on experiencing extreme weather.

# TABLE OF CONTENTS

# STORMY WEATHER

Would you get close to a tornado or thunderstorm? How about fly into a hurricane?

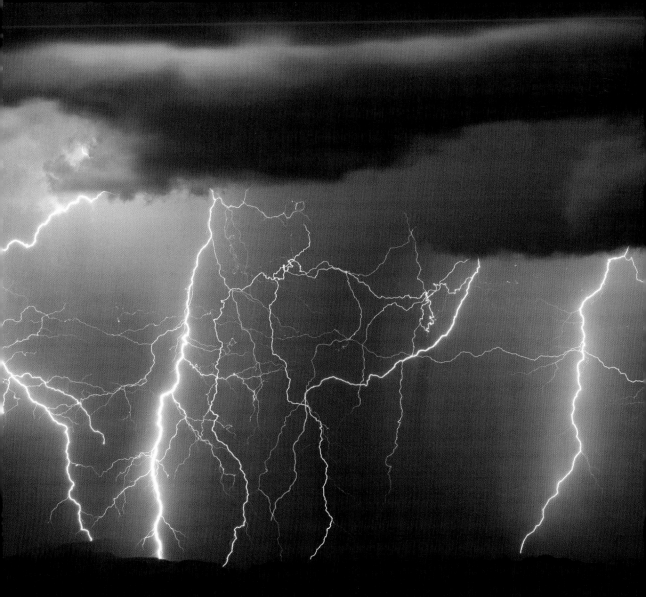

## Thunder and Lightning

There are 16 million thunderstorms worldwide every year! Right now, as you read this, there are 2,000 thunderstorms happening around the world.

Storm chasers study extreme weather events to find out how they work and the direction they are going.

## Saving Lives

Storm chasers track tornadoes and hurricanes. Their knowledge can help save lives.

Tornadoes stretch down from thunderstorms to hit the ground. They range from a few feet to a few miles in **diameter**.

☢ **diameter** (dye-AM-i-tur): a straight line through the center of a circle

Hurricanes are a whirling **cluster** of wind and thunderstorms. The biggest are hundreds of miles across! The strongest hurricanes have wind speeds of more than 154 miles (248 kilometers) per hour.

☢ **cluster** (KLUHS-tur):  to form a group close together

## Caught in the Eye

The eye of a hurricane has very low winds. Birds sometimes get caught in the eye and fly for hundreds of miles until they can fly back out.

# TRACKING
# TWISTERS

No one knows exactly how tornadoes are formed. Storm chasers try to find out.

## Waterspouts

Tornadoes that happen on the water are called waterspouts.

Most storm chasers drive big pickup trucks that can withstand high winds and heavy rain. They also carry cameras and weather **radar** instruments.

 **radar** (RAY-dahr): a way that ships and planes find solid objects by reflecting radio waves off them and by receiving reflected waves

Storm chasers take **measurements** from inside a tornado. This helps experts develop better tornado warning systems.

🔘 **measurements** (MEZH-ur-muhnts): the sizes, weights, or amounts of something

*The TWISTEX storm team, founded by Tim Samaras*

## Tornado Tragedy

Famous storm chaser Tim Samaras died when a tornado suddenly turned toward him in Oklahoma. That's how unpredictable and dangerous tornadoes can be.

Before tornado warning systems, tornadoes such as the St. Louis Tornado (1896) and the Tri-State Tornado (1925) killed and injured thousands. Warning systems give people time to take shelter or get out of a tornado's path.

This image shows the devastation left after a tornado in Joplin, Missouri in 2011.

# HURRICANE
# HUNTING

The National Oceanic and Atmospheric Administration (NOAA) has two planes that fly into hurricanes. They are called Miss Piggy and Kermit.

Scientists in these planes measure wind speed, direction, and temperature. It helps them learn where a hurricane is heading.

When millions in Texas fled Hurricane Rita in 2005, it created a traffic jam that lasted more than 20 hours. Many people died. Knowing a hurricane's direction lets people **evacuate** sooner.

☢ **evacuate** (i-VAK-yoo-ate): to move away from an area because it is or may become dangerous there

40C   (HC)

Interstate 610    WEST

↓ ONLY     ↓

EXIT 40A
Frontage Rd
NEXT RIGHT

(HC)    EXIT 40B

EAST
Interstate 610    TO    TEXAS 225

Pasadena

EXIT ↓ ONLY

SPEED LIMIT 60

23

NOAA hurricane hunters have flown into hurricanes since 1943. There have been some scary moments.

In 1989, a plane flew into Hurricane Hugo and an engine exploded. The pilot flew the plane into the eye and escaped miles later.

# FAMOUS
## STORM CHASERS

The first hurricane hunter was Captain Leonard Povey. In 1935, he flew a plane with an open **cockpit** near a hurricane in the Caribbean Sea. His work helped warn people of the storm's location and direction.

☢ **cockpit** (KAHK-pit): the control center in the front of a plane

The 1935 Labor Day Hurricane badly damaged the Old Bahia Honda Rail Bridge in the Florida Keys.

Emily Sutton started chasing tornadoes in college. Now Emily is a meteorologist. She is also one of the first women to become a famous storm chaser.

*Emily Sutton became KFOR-TV's first female meteorologist in 2009.*

# MEMORY GAME

Can you match the image to what you read?

# INDEX

# SHOW WHAT YOU KNOW

1. What are the names of the NOAA hurricane hunter planes?

2. In what year did Hurricane Rita strike Texas?

3. Who is Emily Sutton?

4. Who flew the first plane to investigate a hurricane?

5. What is a waterspout?

# FURTHER READING

Cordell, Melinda R., *Butterfly Chaos*, CreateSpace Independent, 2016.

Rattini, Kristin Baird, *National Geographic Readers: Weather*, National Geographic Children's Books, 2013.

Squire, Ann O., *Extreme Weather*, Scholastic, 2014.

# ABOUT THE AUTHOR

Kevin Walker has been through many hurricanes, tornadoes, and blizzards. His advice is to learn the science behind weather; it makes it less scary!

**Meet The Author!**
www.meetREMauthors.com

www.rourkeeducationalmedia.com

PHOTO CREDITS: Cover, page 1: ©tobynabours; page 5: ©jerbarber; page 6, 12: ©Beyondimages; page 8: ©crisserby; page 11: ©whiteson; page 11a: ©Harvepino; page 13: ©ellepistock; page 17: ©TonyLaubach; page 19: ©eyecrave; page 20, 22, 24: ©NOAA; page 23: ©Ed Edahl / FEMA; page 26: ©Meinzahn; page 28: ©Adam Murphy

**Edited by:** Keli Sipperley
**Cover and Interior design by:** Rhea Magaro-Wallace

**Library of Congress PCN Data**

Storm Chasers / Kevin Walker
(Daring and Dangerous)
ISBN 978-1-64369-068-1 (hard cover)
ISBN 978-1-64369-071-1 (soft cover)
ISBN 978-1-64369-214-2 (e-Book)
Library of Congress Control Number: 2018955875

Rourke Educational Media
Printed in the United States of America,
North Mankato, Minnesota